I AM PHOENIX

Poems for Two Voices

Also by Paul Fleischman

Picture Books
Time Train
Shadow Play
Rondo in C
The Birthday Tree

Novels
Bull Run
The Borning Room
Saturnalia
Rear-View Mirrors
Path of the Pale Horse
The Half-A-Moon Inn

Short Story Collections
Coming-and-Going Men: *Four Tales*
Graven Images: *Three Stories*

Poetry
Joyful Noise: *Poems for Two Voices*
I Am Phoenix: *Poems for Two Voices*

Nonfiction
Townsend's Warbler
Copier Creations: *Using Copy Machines to Make
Decals, Silhouettes, Flip Books, Films, and Much More!*

I AM PHOENIX

Poems for Two Voices

PAUL FLEISCHMAN

illustrated by Ken Nutt

A Charlotte Zolotow Book

HarperTrophy®
A Division of HarperCollins*Publishers*

I Am Phoenix: Poems for Two Voices
Text copyright © 1985 by Paul Fleischman
Illustrations copyright © 1985 by Ken Nutt
Manufactured in China. For information address
HarperCollins Children's Books, a division of
HarperCollins Publishers, 195 Broadway,
New York, NY 10007.

Library of Congress Cataloging-in-Publication Data
Fleischman, Paul.
    I am phoenix.
    "A Charlotte Zolotow book."
    Summary: A collection of poems about birds to be read
aloud by two voices.
    1. Birds—Juvenile poetry. 2. Dialogues.
3. Children's poetry, American. [1. Birds—Poetry.
2. American poetry] I. Nutt, Ken, 1951–   ill.
II. Title.
PS3556.L422812 1985   811'.54   85-42615
ISBN 0-06-021881-9
ISBN 0-06-021882-7 (lib. bdg.)
ISBN 0-06-446092-4 (pbk.)

21 SCP 20
Designed by Constance Fogler
First Harper Trophy edition, 1989.

For Charlotte, *rara avis*

CONTENTS

NOTE

The following poems were written to be read aloud by two readers at once, one taking the left-hand part, the other taking the right-hand part. The poems should be read from top to bottom, the two parts meshing as in a musical duet. When both readers have lines at the same horizontal level, those lines are to be spoken simultaneously.

I AM PHOENIX

Poems for Two Voices

Dawn

At first light the finches
are flitting about the trees

Flittering

fluttering

flit

purple finches

flit

Fluttering

flittering

fly

painted finches

fly.

Weaver finch
goldfinches

Weaver finch

goldfinches

finches

flit

brown-capped rosy finch

flutter

flit

finches.

Cassin's finch

house finches

flit

finches

flit

flutter

flit

flutter

flit

finches.

Morning

One waxwing's wakened

two   two

rails have risen

three   three

                      teal

four   four

storks

five   five

                      stilts

six   six

California condors

                      seven sleek

seven sleek   trumpeter

                      swans

eight scaups

nine snipes

ten shrikes

twelve

twelve

rufous-sided towhees

fifteen

fifteen

magnificent

magnificent

frigatebirds

frigatebirds

twenty terns

thirty-five

dazzling

dazzling

lazuli buntings

fifty ruffs

sixty wrens

seventy-seven

sea gulls

sea gulls

saviors of

Salt Lake City

Salt Lake City

eighty grouse

ninety grebes

one hundred

one hundred

chickadees!

chickadees!

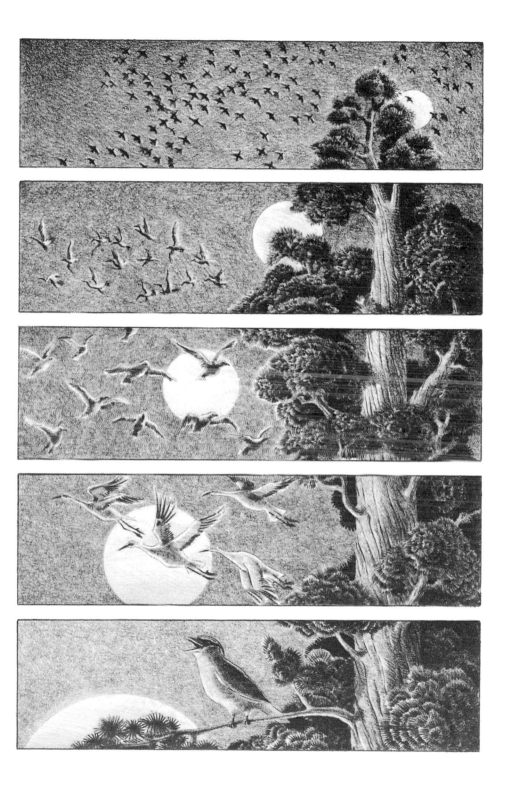

The Wandering Albatross

Behold the wandering
albatross!
Roaming the lonely
oceans

Believed to bear
the souls of lost
mariners

wandering albatross
Men lost to
storms and sharks

Behold the wandering
albatross!

albatross
wandering

wandering
Sailors swept overboard
wandering albatross

albatross roaming

arisen

a-soaring

Albatross!
Wandering
albatross
Wandering
wandering
albatross!

albatross roaming
The shipwrecked

The storm-drowned

Albatross!
Wandering
ceaselessly
journeying

Wandering
albatross!

The Actor

I
seem

seem
a shrike

I
ape

ape
the gull

I
sing just like

sing just like
the cardinal.
I

mimic
coots

mimic

I

mirror
crows

mirror

imitate
the orioles.
I
copy

I
echo

I know by heart

But all of that

sham

is what
I *am.*

I
imitate

copy
wrens

echo
owls
I know by heart
the catbird's calls.

is simply
sham
For a mockingbird

I *am.*

The Watchers

Overhead vultures fly

Peregrine falcons fly

Pigeon hawks
sparrow hawks
red-tailed hawks
sharp-shinned hawks

Black hawks
slowly circling
Marsh hawks

down

Overhead vultures fly

Peregrine falcons fly

Pigeon hawks
sparrow hawks
red-tailed hawks
sharp-shinned hawks

circling
Black hawks

Marsh hawks
peering
down

	at the
ground	ground
	with
great	great
interest.	interest.

The Passenger Pigeon

We were counted not in

                thousands

nor

                millions

but in

billions.   *billions.*

                We were numerous as the

stars   stars

                in the heavens

As grains of

sand   sand

at the sea

                    As the
buffalo   buffalo
                    on the plains.

When we burst into flight
                    we so filled the sky
that the
sun   sun
was darkened
                    and
day   day
                    became dusk.
Humblers of the sun Humblers of the sun
we were!   we were!
The world
inconceivable   inconceivable
                    without us.

Yet it's 1914,
and here I am
alone   alone
                    caged in the Cincinnati Zoo,
the last
                    of the passenger pigeons.

The Common Egret

---

common

Common!

As if to be so white that
snow

clouds

that milk

rates as ordinary.

They call us
common
egrets.

The injustice!

snow
is filled with envy
clouds
consumed with spite
that milk
should seem molasses

Gold   Gold
should be so slandered
diamonds   diamonds
scorned as worthless
rubies   rubies
spurned
                              if common
egrets   egrets
                              are but

common.   *common.*

(*22*)

The Phoenix

I am Phoenix

Phoenix
everlasting!
I am Phoenix!

Immortal
eternal.
I live in
Arabia

eagle
My feathers are
scarlet,
purple,

I am Phoenix
the fire-bird!
Phoenix

I am Phoenix!
Immortal
eternal
undying.

Arabia
I'm as large as an
eagle

scarlet,

golden.

one

there have never been more.
I am my own
daughter
granddaughter
great-granddaughter
I was

will be
my gravedigger.

I gather up twigs of
sweet-smelling spices
and build a nest
on the top of a palm.

Then I wait for noon—

fire
I flap my wings

purple.
There is but
one
Phoenix—

I am my own
mother
grandmother
great-grandmother.
I was
my own midwife,
will be

For each time I discover
I'm becoming old

sweet-smelling spices

I climb inside.

and when the sun's hot as
fire

burst
into flames

which I fan
with my wings
and fan

and I

Eight days pass.
The ashes cool.

in the morning,

just as the sun

I rise
from the ashes
and fly upward—

new

till the twigs beneath me
burst

which I fan
with my wings
and fan
and fan
till the fire

are no more.

Eight days pass.

Then, on the ninth day

at dawn,

rises in the east
I rise

a
new
Phoenix,

my own

mother   daughter

grandmother   granddaughter

great-grandmother   great-granddaughter

and on

and on   and on

until the end of time.   until the end of time.

Warblers

Warblers
warbling

Nashville
warblers

Townsend's
Myrtle
Mourning
Wilson's
warblers

Yellow-
throated

Warblers
warbling

Nashville
warblers

Townsend's
Myrtle
Mourning
Wilson's
warblers

Yellow-
throated

Chestnut-
sided

Dozens
of them

Each one
different.

Hooded
warblers

Hermit
warblers

Bachman's
Brewster's
Blue-winged warblers
warbling.

Chestnut-
sided

Dozens
of them

Each one
different.
Hooded
warblers

Hermit
warblers

Bachman's
Brewster's

Blue-winged warblers
warbling.

The Cormorant's Tale

"As free as a bird"

And I choke when I hear it

I'm an old cormorant
That's my man
with the rope

That circles my throat.
Like all cormorants

The skill's in my bones

"As free as a bird"
I've heard my man say

Consider my case.
I'm an old cormorant

Attached to the ring

Like all cormorants
At catching fish I excel

As my owner knows well.

It's a cormorant's life
To dive down—as right now.

I'm a practiced sea-fowl.
But I'm a caught cormorant

And the rings
round our necks

Just to taste is our fate
Though our stomachs
are sore

Then we dive after more.
I'm a cormorant, yes

To be free and unfettered—
As free as a fish.

It's a cormorant's life

I spot a fish and I seize it

But I'm a caught cormorant
—Not the first nor the last—

Stop us eating our catch.
Just to taste is our fate

But *they* take the fish

I'm a cormorant, yes
And I'll tell you my wish:

As free as a fish.

Sparrows

Sparrows everywhere
There's sparrows
everywhere
They're
squabbling
flitting
singing
Sharp-tailed

Henslow's

Lincoln's

Sparrows everywhere
There's sparrows
everywhere
They're
flitting
singing
squabbling

found in marshes

note white eye-ring

fond of thickets

Vesper

                    white tail feathers

                    visible while perching.

Sparrows everywhere   Sparrows everywhere

They're   They're

flying   flirting

chirping   flying

flirting   chirping

                    Seaside

feeds on insects

                    Cassin's

sings in flight

                    Clay-colored

bird of brushland

                    Ipswich

found at dunes from

Cape Cod south to Georgia.

Sparrows

every-   Sparrows

where there's   every-

squabbling   where there's

flitting   squabbling

singing   sparrows

sparrows   flirting

every-
where there's
sparrows
everywhere.

flying
chirping
sparrows
everywhere.

Doves of Dodona

In the country called Greece
We are doves of Dodona

    We are doves of Dodona
    Near the peak
    called Tomarus

All-fathoming birds
Stood the town
called Dodona
Wise doves of Dodona

    All-fathoming birds

    Wise doves of Dodona
    Where our cooing
    for thousands of years
    has been heard.

We still perch in the oaks
Sacred oaks of Dodona

    Sacred oaks of Dodona
    Where the oracle lived

In the holy grove
There the prophetess stood
Ancient trees of Dodona

She pondered their questions
We are doves of Dodona

Unpuzzling birds
We answered with cooing
Sage doves of Dodona

We disclosed dying days
Oracle of Dodona

Dweller among trees
Told the outcomes of wars
Priestess of Dodona

In the holy grove

Ancient trees of Dodona
And received those
who sought
what the future might hold.

We are doves of Dodona
Then posed them to us

Unpuzzling birds

Sage doves of Dodona
Which only she knew
how to translate
to words.

Oracle of Dodona
Answered questions of love

Dweller among trees

Priestess of Dodona
Till Dodona
was abandoned
and the questions ceased.

In the country called Greece
We are doves of Dodona

All-fathoming birds
Stood the town
called Dodona
Wise doves of Dodona

We are doves of Dodona
Near the peak
called Tomarus
All-fathoming birds

Wise doves of Dodona
Where our cooing
for thousands of years
has been heard.

Dusk

<table>
<tr><td>

swifts and swallows
Snapping up insects
swifts and swallows.

Barn swallows
swifts and swallows
Cliff swallows
cave swallows
swifts and swallows

swallows
swift swallows
swift swallows

</td><td>

At dusk there are swallows
swifts and swallows

swifts and swallows.
Barn swallows
bank swallows
swifts and swallows

Cliff swallows
swifts and swallows
Swift and all-swallowing
swallows

swift swallows

</td></tr>
</table>

                                    swift swallows

swift swallows   swift swallows

swift swallows   swift swallows

swift swallows.   swift swallows.

Whip-poor-will

Whip-poor-will
Will who?
Whip-poor-will

Whip-poor-will
But why?
Whip-poor-will

Whip-poor-will

Hawk told crow
down below

whip-poor-will

Whip-poor-will

Whip-poor-will
Will Grime.
Whip-poor-will

Whip-poor-will
His crime.

He stole a stallion,
witnessed by a hawk high up.

whip-poor-will
Crow told owl
in an oak

Owl told thrush
in a bush   whip-poor-will
                                   Thrush told flea

Flea told dog
                                   Dog told master

Whip   Whip
poor   poor
Will.   Will.

Owls

Sun's down,

Sky's dark,

Loons sleeping

Larks sleeping

Black night

Black night
for them,

Bright noon

Bright noon
for owls.

Barn owls

(siskins sleeping)

Barred owls

(phoebes dreaming)

Screech owls

Screech owls

are

        lis-

        ten-

are   ing

lis-

ten-

ing   are

        lis-

        ten-

        ing

Spotted owls

        (sleeping cranes)

Saw-whet owls

        (dreaming quail)

Elf owls   Elf owls

        are

        call-

        ing

are   out

call-

ing

out   are

        call-

        ing

Great gray owls   Great gray owls
are
calling   calling
out
into the night.   into the night.

Paul Fleischman was born in Monterey, California, and grew up in Santa Monica. He attended the University of California at Berkeley and the University of New Mexico in Albuquerque, and now lives in Pacific Grove, California. He is the author of a number of distinguished books for young readers, including the 1989 Newbery Medal-winning *Joyful Noise: Poems for Two Voices*; the Newbery Honor book *Graven Images*; and *The Half-a-Moon Inn*.

Ken Nutt was born and grew up in Ontario. His work has been represented in several one-man shows there, where he has also received numerous grants and awards for excellence. He is the illustrator of several children's books, including *Joyful Noise: Poems for Two Voices* by Paul Fleischman, under the name of Eric Beddows. He currently lives in Stratford.